# Mile Marker Six

*poems by*

# Ana Maria Spagna

*Finishing Line Press*
Georgetown, Kentucky

# Mile Marker Six

## ACKNOWLEDGMENTS

The following poems originally appeared, or are forthcoming, in literary
journals as noted below:

"Winter Hen" in *Ecotone*
"Ode to a Second Baseman" in *Pilgrimage*
"Somewhere North of the Lost Coast" in *Bellingham Review*
"Shirley Chisholm Dances Salsa in My Dreams" in *What Rough Beast*
"That Night" in *Spoon River Poetry Review*
"Ghost Cub" and "Glue Lam" in *North Dakota Quarterly*

With special thanks to Carol Ann Davis. I would have never dared try
writing poems had I not landed in your workshop. I am forever grateful.

Publisher: Leah Huete de Maines
Editor: Christen Kincaid
Cover Art: Nancy Barnhart
Author Photo: Nancy Barnhart
Cover Design: Elizabeth Maines McCleavy

Order online: www.finishinglinepress.com
also available on amazon.com

Author inquiries and mail orders:
Finishing Line Press
PO Box 1626
Georgetown, Kentucky 40324
USA

# Table of Contents

If You Think the Way to Learn................................. 1

Winter Hen................................................................. 3

The Wanting ............................................................. 5

Shirley Chisholm Dances Salsa in My Dreams ................. 6

Rock Work as Punctuation........................................ 7

That Night................................................................. 9

Sun-Washed Blue: a Memoir ......................................... 10

Fun Run ................................................................... 11

North Rim, 1978 ..................................................... 14

Solitaire................................................................... 16

Redwood from Burnside ............................................. 17

Somewhere North of the Lost Coast............................... 19

Ode to a Second Baseman.......................................... 20

Plantar Fasciitis or What I Fear Most ............................ 21

Power Out................................................................ 23

Eclipse .................................................................... 24

Ghost Cub................................................................ 25

Glue Lam ................................................................. 27

Cosmology of November at Mile Marker Six................. 28

Lemon Cake ............................................................. 29

**If you think the way to learn**

a particular skill, how
to adjust the brakes on a ten-speed
bike from the eighties, say, or how to
layer the beaten eggs, whites and yolks
separated then mixed into a relleno
casserole for which you roasted and peeled
pasillas with a propane torch
in the snow, or how to patch
the ripped side seam on a day pack
you've worn on skis more days
than you've attended faculty meetings
or even, by now, Sunday Mass,
with nylon saved from a windbreaker
with a Boeing insignia or, more crucially,
how to soothe a fussy baby, not your
own, by bounce-stepping through the kitchen
and dining room of your mother's home,
the home you grew up in, a museum
of your happy youth, a place to practice
motherhood—though you'll never be a mother—
or all-purpose nurture, if you
think there's a YouTube video
or even a how-to-manual,
a cloth-covered treasure discovered
in a bookstore downstairs in Pioneer Square
in Seattle, a first edition from 1927
with pen and ink drawings, fine sketches
of the necessary hand tools to stop the wind,
the static car door shock,
black grit wailing, Dad's Pinto paint
job ruined once, pocked, scabbed, somewhere
near Indio, the calligraphied names
like a secret password or handshake,
entry to a club of privilege, not exactly,
but superiority, if you believe, even,
such skills arise like shifting
landforms or seeds in well-tended
soil, then how can we explain
the stop-time moment when, at dusk,
you take aim and hurl a poorly inflated
basketball at the hoop affixed to the gutter

above the garage door at your mother's
house, your old house, and watch
it swish through net alone, what
do you call that?

**Winter Hen**

Seventeen hens, two ducks, a goose, all prime
laying age, well fed and warm. But when you check the coop
on the coldest day of the year

only one sits on eggs, a dozen or more,
her feathers—sunlight through agate, a child's brown hair
summer-streaked—fluffed

wide as a poncho or a wall tent poorly staked.
Her beak faces backward. Steadfast.
But why? Ponds of the future,

says the radio voice, will have fewer tadpoles. Cascade
frogs are in peril, salamanders, newts, all the amphibians.
Pikas, too, we know. And wolverines.

Pines will succumb to spruce bud worm
and drought. House cats will be picked off one by one
by cougars or coyotes.

The hen holds her own, a single cubby in a pen sided
with roofing, hippie-painted, warmed
by a single bulb. Around her, other hens peck

piss-soaked hay, and the goose pins a duck
to the ground by the beak from plain meanness. Sure, bungee
the door tight if you want. The water drip

still freezes overnight. If I could, I'd hire this hen
to copy-edit my grocery list, to mediate
the Democratic caucus, to offer color commentary

on a silver confirmation ring re-sized and relegated,
for good, to the pinky place. If I could, I'd choose
tall socks and vigilance. In the silent woods,

pitch seams plead for fire. Boot tracks
fill with graupel in your wake. The deep snow
soaks clucks and kadoodles

as you trundle toward yellow windows and cradle
in your mittens a cardboard crate of still-warm eggs.

When flakes land on it, they melt.

## The Wanting

The wanting lies flat as farmland
newly shorn, the sharp stalks diminished
while big trucks, other lives, charge past
on dubious missions,
inches from centerline,
and farther on, past winter wheat
a small town, a small house,
single-serving steamed broccoli,
a jogger on the sidewalk slows
to a walk to put her hair in a clip
and in the coulees, rubble accrues,
cliffs obscure the late day light
like loss, columnar basalt cracks and falls.
But still! The red tail grips her post, talons curled,
stoic grace, watching.
And there? There? The mighty Columbia slips
past one dam and the next—14 in all—
her surface so serene you'd never guess she
holds volumes, weight and force
enough to crack concrete
and flood the scablands again. As if to say:
To hell with the ocean. Just let me seep once more
into silt and loess.

## Shirley Chisholm Dances Salsa in My Dreams

The earth's mantle sloshes
under the weight
of a sewing needle      the way
she swivels and dips
chamomile smooth      the way
a callused thumb slips
under apathy      the way
McGregor Mountain glows      the way
a varied thrush sings
the same shrill
note, over and over, as your hips
slide the soft mattress slope.

She shuffles and shimmies
unbought and unbossed, as ever,
and with a cat-eye wink
and a bullhorn she sews
stone shards of my heart
as my legs swing in unison
and my bare feet hit the cold floor
and dust rises in a dump truck's wake
without grace, maybe, but just
enough tenacity.

I'm telling you:
Fighting Shirley taught us
the United States of America
wears gaunt over time
honyocked by rain,
but once unweighted rises again
impervious to pierce      the way
ice cracks granite    the way
pumice floats      the way
plum jam crushes punditry
every time, sin ganas,
and cries for justice,
            sloshing slow.

## Rock work as punctuation

You mix mortar in a wheelbarrow—sand, lime, cement,
then kneel with a trowel, a stack of stones or
several scattered. Here where ancient roots used to hold

soft duff. Thick moss used to cover the boulders
beside the house. Glacial erratics from somewhere
far or native rock from the mountains

above? No way to know. Afternoon wind now stirs
dust exposed during construction, a half-dozen
years back, and swivels the treetops

and the bare foundation waits for someone to choose
new stones. This one for its color. The next for its bevel
or slope or curl or slash. You live staccato.

With a butter knife you learn to smooth the seams.
You bend the tip to fine-tooth the in-between.
Here comes the heavy equipment operator, dimpled

and wry. Hurry as much as you can, he says. The gibe
doesn't stick; you can't revise rock. Walls take years.
Here come coyote pups so small they hide

under leaves of Oregon Grape. Mortar hardens
on your unbuttoned cuffs and your toes cramp
in bent boots. Stop to watch as the pups, all insolence,

nose into rattlesnake weeds. If only you had a camera!
Or better yet! If only you dared stretch your
lower back. Consider the options:

Green, lichen-stained, or oxidized red? Here comes a black
pair of ravens squawking: Rock! Rock! Rock!
The only way is to deviate, to add

thin slices of obsidian. Trucks without mufflers
downshift on the gravel road. Planes trace cotton
lines across a cloud-spattered sky. Baby grouse glean

elderberry seeds from under pink currant
bushes buried long before the last snow
—but mortar holds rock. Full stop.

## That Night

Remember the night
the butcher, the baker, the candlestick maker
rowed the moon boat over the mountains
and we watched from a treeless knob below Purple Pass
and stayed up all night, so so cold,
single digits at least
and shared a trash bag bivvy

industrial strength,
swiped from the compactor
and shivered tooth rattle hard
me in my ragg wool sweater
you with actual down
and the lake sparkled below, a silver fish

shiny-scaled, flipping its gills
down in the dark where red antennas
grace gneiss walls, outsized
and ancient-strange. The others had left us
for quitters. So we stabbed our skis
in ice like a moon-glinted cage—
so we wouldn't slide off
the mountain. We read aloud
to each other from a borrowed
book stories of other mountain
people, able neighbors from
a gentle north. We watched
the moon crest mountains
like waves—Castle, Devore, Tupshin, Bonanza.
Never sinking low nor shooting high
balanced thin and teetery, bright marvel
like those old telemark
boots we found used—and who knew?—they fit.
It must be aliens, we decided
and wriggled from the bag to hop
and holler. Take us! we cried. Take us!

On cold nights afterwards—for years—we'd ask one other: what if
that night we'd leapt aboard? Then at some point,
we knew: We did.

## Sun-washed Blue:  A Memoir

Sky like a salt bath, like a Polaroid unshook—washed
like seduction, the fjord horses paw hard cool dirt

by the hitchrail the seeps and blades
green and yellow enough to run my fingers over

like a shaven skull. Never a horse girl
no statues sleek or stocky named then ignored

instead St. Francis faceless with five doves glazed dull tan
sits on the bookcase, a gift from Father Charlie

when I was five. How do we carry these things,
five clay doves clattering against our ribs like wooden boats

launched in the irrigation ditch? When he broke
how I howled. In a tentless bag, I rustle

autumn sedge beneath scattershot stars
while the animals huff and knock dry earth

like prayer tuned to sinew and grit
and at dawn egg shells settle coffee grounds

in an aluminum pot. What if it'd been a Palomino
or a Morgan, Arabian, Appaloosa, or god,

I could never keep track of proper girl frills
or crushes or horsey fantasies—would I cling so hard?

Probably not. I mean, even Father Charlie didn't stay a priest
for long. Tomorrow: a nosebleed, dust,

warm horse breath, home. You glued him whole
and put him back on the shelf next to Daisy, the cat,

a decade gone, and a white skeletal jaw,
a rodent maybe, or a fawn,

and the bird book we never use, its cover faded,
over time, to sun-washed blue.

**Fun Run**

In Rancho Cucamonga
on a Saturday
we went to a fun run,
my dad and me.
The park was empty
so early, and the grass
was dead, but the sky
had this soft white
on the blue that brought to mind
a Monkees song. The runners
arrived. They stretched
their quads and calves.
Nikes and Adidas,
nylon shorts and loose
tanks with team names
like Rialto Roadrunners,
and Loma Linda Lopers.
My dad went to sign us up
got numbers to safety
pin on our shirts.
I'd never used
a safety pin myself, something
I knew I should know
at eight, but when I tried to get Dad
to help he'd gone.

Colored flags marked
the finish. Red, yellow, blue.
Radio music played loud.
KISS FM. Billy Joel or maybe
Elton John. I stood alone
with four safety pins
by folding tables
with blue water jugs
and plates of orange slices.
I held the paper number wide
as my waist in my left hand
and the open safety
pin in my right. A woman with thin
muscles and a jutted jaw
exactly like Mickey Dolenz

stood near me,
and I hoped she'd see I was
the youngest after all,
and a girl besides.
I stood out. I could act
helpless, I knew.
This dumb number! But
just thinking that
made me feel
ashamed.

With ten minutes 'til start time, I walked
a little way apart. Under a pepper
tree I listened to the radio blare
some thick milk voice but my song
was better, I knew. The Monkees'
song soared in me like something
I owned, a morning anthem
strong as white blue sky
and pepper tree smell, it beat
against my ribs, mixed with the sweat
and huff of all these runners.
I bounced on my toes on bare dirt
just off the dead grass
ready.

When Dad returned, he smiled
to show that one missing tooth.
If he'd worried, it did not show.

With one hand on my back he urged me
to the start. My number in place—
who knows how—
the cold pin rubbed the skin
on my chest. Bare legs
crowded round, hairy thick,
tangled tense, bulging. I toed
the chalk at the start. The gun
went off. I ran on the
edge of the pack
of bodies and Dad's

hairy back got lost
somewhere—

But that one song?
The guitars jangled like bells
in my mind with voices chiming
*it could be done so easily*
*you didn't know*
voices rose and drums,
guitars like bells
like the cross atop
Mt. Rubidoux
in the white blue morning
louder than
the loudspeaker, the start gun,
my fast feet slapping
dead grass, louder than
shame. And I felt
my body.
I knew for sure
all it could be.
I knew right then:
That's all you ever need
in Rancho Cucamonga
on a Saturday in
October 1978.

### North Rim, 1978
*—after Frank Bidart*

What I hope (when I hope) is for a space
like the way back—

… a moving PRISON

in which we passed miles
so bored, god so bored

TRAPPED in moving TRAPPEDNESS

… for like the Bradys on mules (a green Volvo)
in the Grand Canyon

once we'd been jostled by the road

we beseeched the sky, the billowing
thunder fat clouds

for a cymbal, a shock, a shout

to switch the channel from
reruns long-memorized

theme songs in scenery

(the soaring strains, pre-packaged
override the strains we hear)

that is the REFRAIN within the REFRAIN

TRAPPED in moving TRAPPEDNESS

… there will be (yet unseen) years when I
abandon, deny,

if not quite betray you—; before credits roll

a diagnosis, not yet dire, and your texts
haphazard and ungrammatically

late, pleading but not pleading

burnt like gas fumes we breathed
in; achy; nauseous

This is the knowing of the danger of the sky

while the sky was alert;—grief,
omens, foreshadowings of botched escape

not made (though ready) for prime time

TRAPPED in moving TRAPPEDNESS

… for there's a way despite motion, we still
inhabit the secret place together…

… whether hope or delusion, just this

To be with you: two girls riding unbelted
in a green Volvo, looking back.

## Solitaire

The blue veins on the back of her hands
slip over tendons thin as twigs.
She holds a cigarette in her left, True Blue brand,
pinched tight, and with the right, slaps
playing cards, one on the next, her downward
gaze—half-here, half-not—like her one lazy eye
brown as a Folgers can or her gray-black curls.
She lines cards in unruly rows, until she's stumped
or triumphs, then she gathers them up with the help
of her cigarette hand—ring finger and pinky—
drags them back into a stack.

I'd quit if I could, she says. I've tried.

She turns over the three of clubs,
flicks her ash, checks the clock on the wall,
not yet time for Shake n' Bake or mostaccioli
for four, not five. While other kids ride bikes
over hardpan ditches, I sit at the kitchen table,
wave my blue ribbon for spelling, say, or jump rope
or god knows what—yet another—between my thumb
and index finger, nails gnawed, ever-hopeful
to break this solitaire spell, or hold on forever.

That's nice, honey, she says.

Someday we'll fly to Cancun, just us two.
We'll wade water blue as silk, tour
sun-splintered ruins, sip café con leche in the plaza,
with bougainvillea draped over stucco, and ride a too-crowded
ferry through choppy seas. Our bodies tossed together
hard at the dock, I'll reach for that same
blue vein hand, neither of us old yet, exactly—not yet—
but also not young.

At dusk, in a fan-cooled motel, we'll play gin rummy
and keep score on a coach-class ticket.

**Redwood from Burnside**

The redwood fence we climbed
til it sagged shuddering
bolts loose like baby teeth

Painted red, too—confusingly—
by the two orange trees
oranges rotting green

Thin wide boards and skinny
arms, a barking mutt, a mulberry
tree with hard-pruned

Limbs that reach past
the railing, thick and impudent,
where we hide, as they say, in plain

Sight from mid-day sun,
not so different, really,
from this redwood town

Shuttered by septic gone foul,
a blue tarp corseted to his bike,
sword ferns in the spokes,

A lone bare-chested hippie rides the
white line unsteadily thru
slug trails in the mirror while

Somewhere in the forest, a small child
ducks into a fallen log, hollowed not
bucked. Like art, she cries, like art!

Redwoods shade encroachers and grow
green cones at rarified heights. Red fungi
rise bulbous from wet duff.

Say what you will about
tide-strewn urchins,
or Visqueen driftwood-pinned.

Here, light streams elsewhere
always, not on you—
& what relief!

## Somewhere North of the Lost Coast

You drove this way once and found God, or re-found
Him (and who wouldn't?)
a splintered table, through-bolted, and the wide Pacific,
gray clouds layered three fingers thick atop. If you were here,
you'd carry a bucket and a heavy rod
to the surf edge and cast long.
I drove this way once, alone, the most alone
I'd ever been. Elatedly alone, I mean, not beholden
nor even seen, wet cloud transcendence
shrouded the last rise through trees
and a kind of terror rose in me not unlike, maybe—
finding God. Listen, those black mussels
I watched you pry apart. I didn't know
the orange inside was a living thing, only studied
your meaty hands, hair beneath the knuckle,
splitting it rough down the middle, tossing the sharp shell aside.
You slid the flesh over the barb. Once, on a beach like this,
I fucked a man who was afraid to cross bridges.
When we drove away sated, the stars opulent,
garish, we stopped at each river to switch. Why,
I wonder, didn't I drive the whole time?

The surf retreats then returns. Try to fuck away
the tenderness, try to cloud-bury the blue;
a hard callous builds under a silver ring,
around the bend from redwood burl stands—
buy old weathered wood here!
I do. I did. I will. I can't help it.
At the visitor center down the road
a photo shows a Yurok woman
with a sixty pound salmon on her back—sixty!
and the ranger says a gray whale swims just offshore
in the fog. Guess we won't see her today, I say.
He shrugs: it could burn off.

When I try to say what's been lost
where clouds swab the tree fringe
Not sad, I say, more like halved.
Black shells litter the sand.
I'd tug you from the line stretched thin to show you:
Look, now, how lovely, the silver-blue inside

If you were here.

## Ode to a Second-Baseman

His shoulders were blue heeler haunches.
His biceps were glacial moraines.
His right wrist was a bat broken
on a first pitch,
and his left was a Fresno afternoon.
His fingers were an archipelago,
and the skin on the back of his hands was orange peel
or maybe paper bark.

His mouth was honey and vinegar
in a thermos lid,
and his teeth were bushtits on a lazy doe's back.
His voice was cedar duff
and his whistle was eucalyptus.

And his eyes were blue oil paint
And his anger was a felt pen smudge
And his cough was ice slabs crashing from frozen falls
And his last days were cracked dirt on a ballfield.

His wit was a fielder's glove well-oiled.

If I hadn't seen the bag zipped shut,
I wouldn't believe.
Because I always throw myself
hardest at now.

**Plantar Fasciitis or What I Fear Most**

The tendon taut in my right arch, a sharp
tug, a kind of mid-step tear, a stab
of pain with potential to stop
my training cold—
even though I roll my foot
over frozen orange juice in a can,
suspend my heel from a carpeted stair
to stretch my calf, empty the Costco bottle
of ibuprofen, all 500 tablets.
It's happened before.

Gail, who ran thirty miles
from a wedding by a high lake,
three years later—hobbled for good,
Janet, three botched surgeries
in, can't do triathlons any more,
not ever. And you,
that time you knifed
the Achilles of a logging boot
to relieve pressure, when all you
needed was rest.

Or maybe it's the way big-heartedness
washes over me in the woods
or waist deep in water, any water,
knocks me desperate with desire
to swaddle the whole world,
and at the same time, terrified
that I'll bungle the job, suffocate
the bigness with banalities, or simply forget
what it meant.

Or this, this, of course: when you're
gone, and the sky turns on me,
like my feet (don't fail me now) when race
day nears, and nothing's left, nothing at all,
not the daughter we never had (we forgot)
no bright shreds of you left:
useless with a calendar, say, deft
with her hands, prone to joint pain,
and exuberant silliness.

On the gravel, I tune myself
to my right arch, gauging, and don't notice
new willows or puffballs on the berm,
thunderheads building over Boulder Creek,
or anyone waving. You never look up, you say,
and laugh, thank god, as you sponge
coffee grounds from the counter. You'll miss
my inattention someday. And me,

I'll wish I'd stopped
running altogether and stayed in bed
instead to listen for the weather forecast
even though it's almost always wrong.

**Power Out**

The battery backup beeps
sharp and insistent
rhythmic outage every morning
when ice clogs the hydro.

I used to drill boulders for the PUD.
Pinned and rigged, they dangled
from cable over water
to shore to clear the input.

One day I slipped too close
to the small opening, round
and just big enough for me
to slide down the steel pipe
to the needle valve and turbine
to power overhead lights and
text messages from grown
children, oven-
roasted potatoes, and
heat tape in the crawl space.

You'd go to dirt anyway, why not electricity?

But no, I'd only clog it up
stopper the system, require a welder's
torch, rescue helicopters,
my poor mother's grief.

And anyway he grabbed me in time,
a man born on my 23rd birthday,
soft bearded and strong,
a one-armed yank. I fell
on the rocks drill still in hand.
The lights flicker on.

## Eclipse

                   Don't look directly;
look through a pinhole or dark paper specs,
look at others not looking, but not too long
(don't stare!) at smooth skin, mounded and sunk,
whiskered maps to new eras. Even the sun goes blind
or maybe she doesn't know,
still imagines herself photosynthesizing
as saucers tip to spill
time in the corner of a warped skillet
or a leashed dog's eye.
                   You could be in Madras
for full dark or elsewhere on the right track,
stopped in road-strewn thistle
and wildfire, as the moon, second
fiddle so long, steps up with giddy glory to scallop
the sidewalk with self-portraits. You've wrong-
tracked (delightedly) so long you're shocked
by soft care now for the unsighted.
                   Nothing she's done wrong, nothing at all,
just the moon, sly as a saddle sore, spinning sunlight
into slivers.

## Ghost Cub

Once I saw a dead cub floating near shore, free of fur
        but still flesh, a transparent apparition. I couldn't tell if she fell, spooked,
          or wounded first, she slid.
Where else can they go?
(Where, for that matter, can any of us?)

In a speedboat's wake the ghost cub rose and fell, upright
            in a way, like a small child crawling on her hands and knees in
        supplication or (vain) escape.

We fed mouse click fodder to the gods, slept like sugar ants sticky
        on the counter, wandered alone, tender flesh, and more than once
                      succumbed, gladly.
Let them in! (I'm scared)
My neighbors say no. (They're scared.)

Once in the woods, I came upon a dead chicken, still feathered, hung from a
limb
            over loaves of Wonder Bread, still wrapped and on fire,
        in a shallow pit. Or I should say, smoldering.

Bear bait, the ranger told me. Don't you know?

(This is not ours!)

... a hard pew, a hand recorder, an agenda, Ecclesiastes or Acts,
an organ velvet-draped beneath the Power Point
               —or else a torn warning from a trailhead.

How rarely, now, we drop to our knees: to scrub the floor
      with a dirty sponge, to wrap heat tape on pipes in the crawl space, to try
        (vainly) to protect what's ours.

(None of it is ours!)

Mud bees nest in knotholes under the eaves and 3/8th screw holes
        on the boombox casing; the rifle was bought legally,
the suspect appears to be
            in a state of shock.

When the wake rolled smooth, the cub tipped from sight.

The sick silence of what we knew, but didn't know.

(What of it is ours?)

## Glue Lam

they say will delaminate
over time the seams will separate
integrity fail
      a single beam one log one tree
shaved to its core as if skewed  vertebrae
could yet shoulder regret
      the trees we felled
      the money unspent
on high dollar pressed board equations
blinkering in blue light shipped from afar—a made thing
      instead this two-topped tree
enough by measure but dried
impatiently when the boom truck
puts it in place
      to gaze at clear grain
with clear envy or who am I kidding
      a tailored canker with pleats
      a clear pane of prose
      a steel plate fashioned at Kelly's
Iron Works with a torch and drill to scratch pad dimensions
these six bolts black threaded
      hold straight~ or straight enough
      and brace the galaxy in parallel lines
while the barrel stove pings diesel-soaked planer
shavings like carrot peels stretch steel to unseal
the unused power stored in heavy batteries out back

## Cosmology of November at Mile Marker Six

A well-drained conversation
Splayed on old snow: silver, then black
Like a Dodge down-shifting, or silent

As the pepper of constellations
Under bedcovers. You were dropped cog by cog,
A parachute lifted by labor.

Other times, your shoulder blades filed
Sharp to split the connotation
You tried to run seeds

Through an electronic sieve
And measure the weight of possessives
In the so-called Cloud

Growing stale, waiting
For progress, waiting for the curdled
Rasp, the second  act, from which

Sculpted schist ages, like whiskey.
But don't splice your confession; it's fated
To take a fall, to balance

Atmospheric pressure. "Today I rake the lines
Let the dung beetles shift meaning."
A carabineer and her rushed cronies.

The allergies scuttle stove ash
And hard squash apply for amnesty
(Dry soil seduces wind.

If you could translate birdsong
Would I finally shed tears?) and lecture
The power grid, litigated, mitigated

To envision a carburetor
To disengage, to simmer long.

**Lemon Cake**

1.
We crossed the highway bottles in your purse clanking, the sky awash in waves of stars crashing toward the sage sea cliffs. We walked for miles to the cabins long abandoned, and we stood on the once-porch high tide wet and wept and wept wept salt tears past lost beach days, lost days to come, hospital tubes and beeping machine lights ship lights rocking. We lay in the sand heads on each other's shoulders, beer buzzed, walk weary, and remembered how once we ate wet lemon cake from a square pan in the back of a truck on the freeway while traffic raced and our hair whipped salt blond-white, and we draped ourselves in an over-sized cotton sleeping bag and held it on our salt itch thighs, the taste of gasoline and smog grit, our legs tangled our thoughts (non-thoughts) still floating over swells, your head still bobbing sun sick and the cold cold ridges of the pickup dented our flesh until the square pan edges were scraped and cold and stars dusted the sky like powdered sugar just like tonight.


2.


we waited for waves in three-count sets
—as if sets were real—we waited
for the biggest ones begged to get
knocked over hard—we'd all been there

knew the scraped-skin sting
of rising in froth
sand in your crotch and seaweed string
caught under the thin straps

of last year's suit, we stood in the waves
for hours the longest we ever had
or would and weren't quite friends but gave
ourselves this once to the sun

and each other as skin burned
and peeled off our shoulders
like tiny clawed crabs hermits
we fed live to anemones

at home roaches scuttle
and girls toy with brittle hair and

persimmons and warm soda puddles
on the unwatered lawn

but on your 13th birthday
we skewered blue green swells
buoyant emergent as yet unfrayed
at dusk we wore proud scabs


3.

Girls hover in hives, and you slip among them.
The skins of lemons could peel the paint off an Oldsmobile,
phone booth decals, a Tom Petty riff, a casket.


4.

Lemons ripen early.
They hang wet and wait on spiked limbs
to be picked and sacked.

Oranges, too, rot in mid-air.
Flesh turns tart to pulp on the tree
moldy green in the dirt.

Women from church brought hot dishes
and bags of pink grapefruit
we'd never eat.

Pomegranates dropped and stained tile
along Victoria where at 16 a man
threw a brick at my bike.

Black plums grew by the patio, peaches, too—both gone.
Dozers knocked down the groves, yarded
the twisted phone cord through my fingers.

5.

Swallows flit and swerve at dusk
over the surface smooth and green,
so green it belies the cold beneath, so cold.
They're after insects we can't see.

Their flight appears unscripted,
a flash of iridescence when they turn one eighty,
throat to the sky. In fact, it's calculation,
all angles and aim, pre-meditated sparks.

The swallow's side-turned tail feathers
are evasive and sublime.
They nest in mud and wait for the wind to still.

Under the surface, a cutthroat mourns August,
its mouth a punctured leather holster
its gut empty, again, still.

The sun sifts for smoke.
The golden eye trails a veil.
The swallows, once frantic, flail and disperse.

Try to grow a lemon tree in ten feet of snow
or a bonsai tamarack for that matter.
Try to graft a peach to a rose.
Try to split a fir needle lengthwise to spare it harm.

Once we ducked waves.
Now we skim ballast.


6.

Until one night when summer fades
you hear the phone; she hears a loud knock.
The boy sits in the back strapped with cold take-out,
the stars marine blurred. This time you will drive

past Chihuahuas frantic behind closed drapes,
past the stoplight at Phoenix where your father fell
toward Van Buren and the 60, Mt. Baldy
scratched free of snow and smog, this sewage
plant over the dry river, this bamboo
where she hunkers with the wild boars and
shopping carts, teeth bared, now asleep
in the passenger seat, past boys on bikes, knees splayed
to Ave Maria & west toward sand, the curling blue
traffic stopped at the 605. The phone? Never
will stop ringing, a coiled cord
swings from the wall in the bunkhouse,
waiting for you, waiting for scalding coffee
with a flip lid mouth, waiting for someone
to clean, for once, the dog shit
off the carpet. Your father runs
somewhere, his chest shaved bare; it itches
bad when it grows; she picks windshield
from her forehead. That field plowed to chunks?
Where some kids built bike jumps, never us?
That field is on fire. The boy in the back stuffs
tangled cords into a nest of bleached detonation
and begs to buried again in sand.


7.


You can never be sure. A freeway
overpass (or a runner) can collapse. As oranges
sweeten, you may flee,

Or you may love a woman whose bare toes
curl over chair rungs in the kitchen.
She held you straight and you bend.

Or you may flip off
the uneven bars, nail the dismount
speed east over the Badlands to the Mojave.

You've tired of waiting.
You want to burn the tarmac

& everything is tarmac.

At last, you accelerate into glass
shatter past prickly pear where
hitchhikers hold their thumbs low.


8.


I meet my sister at this Salvadoran joint
she knows in Duarte.
I offer her seeds.
She offers me gas money
and a plastic comb.
Gol! Says the TV again. Gol!
This is just how it went down
when we were small:
a long drive in heat, a burger
on a spongy bun, with guacamole,
and Fleetwood Mac, a friend from church
with the car keys.
Empanadas bled on the table.
She offered to make calls
and collect Mom's
three night gowns
but could not hold still
and any way
if you don't hit the road by three,
you might as well stay.


9.


Someone will find me where I was hiding
behind ice blocks meant to slide over grass hills
with stars at my feet rising

like pipe smoke or Nagahyde worn by love
from the soft owl's face; Kaiser, they whispered;
Kaiser, unseen; the fuselage shudders,

square blocks melt round, and the interstate
knots tight around the house where I brought grapes
to feed grief one by one on a couch

in Corona. Down there somewhere the Pacific
plate rubs hard against the continent, lemon-
scented, ever-shifting on a fault.

Our waves shatter on land.

Ana Maria Spagna is the author of several books including *Uplake: Restless Essays of Coming and Going, Reclaimers,* stories of elder women reclaiming sacred land and water, *Test Ride on the Sunnyland Bus,* winner of the *River Teeth* literary nonfiction prize, *100 Skills You'll Need for the End of the World (as We Know It)* a humor-infused exploration of how to live more lightly on the planet, and two previous essay collections, *Potluck* and *Now Go Home.* Her first novel for young people, *The Luckiest Scar on Earth,* about a 14 year-old snowboarder and her activist father, appeared in 2017. Ana Maria's work has been recognized by the Society for Environmental Journalists, Nautilus Book Awards, and as a four-time finalist for the Washington State Book Award. She lives in the North Cascades. You can find her at www.anamariaspagna.com and on Twitter @amspagna